In Celebration

Our lives are happily interspersed with celebrations. They come in many different forms—a holiday, birthday, wedding, or an anniversary. Be it on a national or family scale, intimate or grand, there is surely no more fitting way of marking it than with a splendid piece of fine celebratory music. Many great composers have written music for such occasions. Listen to the solemnity of Beethoven's *Symphony No.9 in D Minor*, the exaltation of Charpentier's joyous hymn *Te Deum*, the stately rhythms of Chopin's *Military Polonaise,* or the intensity of Verdi's "Triumphal March" from *Aïda*—and rejoice.

THE LISTENER'S GUIDE – WHAT THE SYMBOLS MEAN

THE COMPOSERS
Their lives... their loves.. their legacies...

THE MUSIC
Explanation... analysis... interpretation...

THE INSPIRATION
How works of genius came to be written

THE BACKGROUND
People, places, and events linked to the music

Contents

MARC-ANTOINE CHARPENTIER
c.1634–1704

Te Deum

PRELUDE

The *Te Deum*—or, in its full name, the *Te Deum Laudamus* ("We Praise Thee, O God")—is one of the most uplifting hymns, and Marc-Antoine Charpentier's setting is among the most powerful. It opens with an exultant fanfare, the trumpet soaring high above the orchestra to establish a stately and magnificent theme. This theme is then developed by a series of subtly varied repetitions, with the drums and strings lending eloquent support to the grand opening.

LATIN WORDS

The *Te Deum* is one of the oldest Christian hymns. No one is certain who wrote the original Latin words. It may even be that the text we know today is derived from several different writers. But it appears to have reached its definitive form by the mid-6th century. In Christian churches, the *Te Deum* forms the climax of morning services.

LIFETIME GOAL

Marc-Antoine Charpentier's exact date of birth is in question. While 1634 is the date most often cited, recent scholars suggest that he may have actually been born some ten years later. There is no mystery, however, concerning his death—he died in Paris on February 24, 1704. During his lifetime, he was widely admired but never attained his ambition of an official post at the court of the "Sun King," Louis XIV. This was largely due to his rival, Jean-Baptiste Lully, who enjoyed royal patronage and conspired against him. He did, however, gain an appointment as musician to the king's son, the Dauphin, and the king eventually granted him a pension. As a composer, Charpentier concentrated on music for the stage and, later, on church music. This setting of this *Te Deum*, one of four he is known to have composed, dates from the early 1690s.

Below: *A portrait of Louis XIV and family, including Charpentier's benefactor the Dauphin* (second from right), *by Jean Nocret.*

ANOTHER CHARPENTIER

Though no relation to Marc-Antoine, Gustave Charpentier (1860–1956) *(right)* is best known for his opera *Louise*. He also wrote the popular *Impressions of Italy* while a student under the leading French teacher Jules Massenet.

RELIGIOUS MUSIC

 In the mid-1680s, around the time of the births of J.S. Bach and George Friderick Handel, Charpentier became closely associated with the church of St. Louis in Paris. It was thanks to the power of this influential Jesuit church, which later came to be known as St. Paul-St. Louis, that Charpentier became one of the most important Catholic composers in Europe. Almost all of what remains of Charpentier's religious music

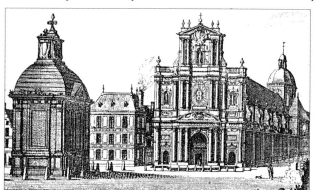

comes from this period, which accounted for the last twenty years of his life. It includes not only his famous *Te Deum*, but also the beautiful *Christmas Midnight Mass* and the *Assumpta est Maria* Mass.

Left: *St. Paul-St. Louis— setting for much of Charpentier's music.*

EUROVISION SONG CONTEST

 Charpentier's *Te Deum* achieved huge popularity when it was adopted by the European Broadcasting Union as the introductory theme for all its Eurovision telecasts in the early 1960s. A recording of this late 17th-century piece of classical music entered the French pop charts and stayed there for many weeks! **EUROVISION**

FRÉDÉRIC CHOPIN *1810–1849*

Polonaise in A Major

No.1, Opus 40, "Military"

Steeped in tradition, this song is often played in Chopin's homeland, Poland, during times of celebration or crisis. The opening theme of this rousing polonaise is among the most famous that he ever wrote. The noble tune that follows maintains the stirring pride and passion of the music, until the opening theme comes striding back to stir the blood of music lovers in Poland and throughout the world.

NATIONAL DANCE

Although Chopin spent most of his life in Paris, he always remained a Polish patriot and had a great fondness for the polonaise—a traditional Polish dance. He wrote sixteen of them, the earliest when he was only seven years old. This one ranks among his finest mature works.

GIUSEPPE VERDI *1813–1901*

ACT 2 (TRIUMPHAL MARCH)

The ceremony of an ancient Egyptian victory parade is expertly recreated as Giuseppe Verdi's grand march opens with a stunning call to arms from massed trumpets. Answered by quieter instruments, the music steadily grows in excitement and intensity until the chorus enters, singing a magnificent hymn of praise. The march surges on its way with various strands combining to make one of the finest of all operatic spectacles, expressed in music of the most intense and memorable quality. A faster section ensues, full of Egyptian bustle, before the majesty of the march finally returns.

THE CAIRO CONNECTION

Toward the end of 1869, when Verdi was fifty-six and at the height of his powers, an Italian opera house was planned to open in Cairo *(right)*. This was the year in which the Suez Canal was opened, and it was decided that Verdi should compose an opera to celebrate both events. Although he accepted the commission from the Khedive of Egypt and chose a story set appropriately in that country's ancient times, the opera, *Aïda*, was not completed until two years later.

Right: *Program to* Aïda *at the Royal Opera House, Covent Garden.*

A CAST OF THOUSANDS

Aïda continues to be one of Verdi's enduring successes yet he wasn't even present at its opening night. Because he was a bad sailor and hated traveling by ship, he refused to make the voyage across the Mediterranean from the southernmost tip of Italy to Egypt where the first production was to take place. Regardless, it was a sensation. Less than two months later, *Aïda* was performed at La Scala in Milan. Verdi *(left, conducting Aïda in Paris)* was present on this occasion and enjoyed one of the biggest successes of his career.

KEY NOTES

The first New York performance of Aïda was in 1873. The British premiere was at the Royal Opera House, Covent Garden, in 1876, with the soprano Adelina Patti making her debut in the role.

7

ROBERT SCHUMANN *1810–1856*

Piano Concerto in A Minor

OPUS 54: THIRD MOVEMENT

The last movement of this joyful Romantic piano concerto greets the listener as a sudden blaze of color, with solo piano taking center stage. A running theme on the piano, with soft orchestral accompaniment, soon leads to the famous marchlike tune, first played quietly on the strings and then taken up by the piano. The sense of celebration is quite infectious.

MUSICAL GIFT

Schumann wrote his *Piano Concerto* for his talented wife, Clara. An influential teacher, as well as a notable composer, Clara went on to become the most important woman pianist of the 19th century. She gave the first performance of the *Piano Concerto* herself on New Year's Day in 1846 and continued to tour and play regularly until her death in 1896, at the age of seventy-seven.

KEY NOTES

This piano concerto originated in 1841, when Schumann wrote a one-movement piece for piano and orchestra called **Phantasie**. Schumann and his wife, Clara, both felt the piece needed expanding and two further movements were added in 1845.

EMMANUEL CHABRIER *1841–1894*

Joyeuse Marche

This boisterous and catchy march opens with a flourish from the full orchestra. This is at once contrasted with music from the woodwind section that leads to a high-spirited theme on the horns. The entire sequence is repeated before a new tune, first heard on the clarinets alone, appears. From then on, new ideas join variants of earlier ones in a display of orchestral virtuosity, before a musical quote from a popular song of the day— *"En rev'nant dans la revue"* ("Returning from the parade")—brings the march to its end.

A LATE START

Emmanuel Chabrier was one of the most influential French composers of the 19th century. Although he did not leave a great deal of music behind, his confident and optimistic style and mastery of orchestration, ensured his place in musical history. Chabrier *(left)* was born in 1841 in central France. At the age of fifteen he moved to Paris and joined the Civil Service, playing the piano *(right)* and composing in his spare time. By his mid-thirties it became clear that his future lay in music. Sadly, however, his career was not a long one, and by his late forties Chabrier had become both mentally disturbed and physically incapacitated. He died at age fifty-three.

ARTISTIC FRIENDS

Once established on the Parisian musical scene, Chabrier began to move in all the leading artistic circles and was a frequent guest at many of the best houses and social affairs. As well as being admired by his musical friends, Chabrier became close to the poet Verlaine, who wrote a sonnet in honor of his friend. Chabrier also admired Impressionism and became a great friend of the artist Manet. Chabrier bought several of his paintings, including "Bar at the Folies Bergere" *(right)*; Manet painted two portraits of the composer.

TEN OPERAS

From Chabrier's ten operas, his two greatest successes were *Gwendoline* in 1886 and *Le Roi malgré lui* in 1887 ("King Despite Himself"). With a libretto by the French writer Catulle Mendès, *Gwendoline (right)* was centered around a love story between the Viking King Harald and a Saxon princess, Gwendoline. The opera was influenced by Richard Wagner—a fact reflected by its initial rejection by the Paris Opera as being "too Wagnerian."

WAGNER'S INFLUENCE

Chabrier's respect for Wagner *(left)* and his music dates back to an 1879 visit to Germany with fellow composer Henri Duparc. Duparc, who was an ardent admirer of Wagner's music, made it his mission to expose Chabrier to the composer's works. Wagner's revolutionary opera *Tristan and Isolde*, in particular, made an indelible impression on Chabrier and he became convinced that composition was his destiny as well. Becoming a keen champion of the German composer's music, Chabrier successfully worked many of Wagner's themes into piano duets.

KEY NOTES

The composition of the Joyeuse Marche dates from 1888 and was originally entitled Marche Française. Along with Chabrier's other orchestral masterpiece, the rhapsody España, it confirms the French composer's place as a forerunner of great French composers such as Debussy and Ravel.

CAMILLE SAINT-SAËNS *1835–1921*

Symphony No.3 in C Minor

OPUS 78, "ORGAN": SECOND MOVEMENT

This majestic symphony reflects a France emerging from the shadow of the Franco-Prussian War. A thunderously full organ chord opens the concluding part of this movement before the strings respond. Then, two pianists quietly trace a delicate path around it, before the organ takes charge again and the theme becomes one of celebration. Emboldened by this, the violins begin a powerful fugue, where the instruments imitate one another. Finally, the brass build a wall of sound in which the theme is intoned by full orchestra.

A LONG AND FRUITFUL LIFE

Saint-Saëns lived a long and fruitful life, dying at the age of eighty-six with over two hundred works to his name. Although published as *Symphony No.3*, and dating from 1886, this is actually the last and finest of the five symphonies he wrote.

ORGAN REVIVAL

In Saint-Saëns's day, the organ was very much a rarity in concert music. Apart from Liszt's *Faust* and *Dante* and Tchaikovsky's *Manfred* symphony, its use in a major symphony was limited. However, the influence of Liszt and the inspiration of the French organ builder Cavaillé-Coll ensured that Saint-Saëns would give it a major role in his epic symphony.

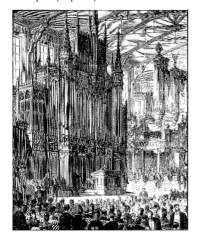

Composers such as Camille Saint-Saëns were inspired by the organs (above) built by the great master Cavaillé-Coll.

IN MEMORY

Symphony No.3 is scored for a large symphony orchestra, incorporating two pianos and an organ. It is dedicated to the memory of Franz Liszt *(right)*, a good friend of Saint-Saëns who had died shortly before the work was finished. In 1871, it was Liszt who ensured the first performance of Saint-Saëns's opera *Samson and Delilah* after it had been rejected in Paris because of its subject matter. Saint-Saëns had always intended to inscribe the symphony to Liszt, whose influence is evident in the work's unusual thematic transformation and novel orchestral effects.

KEY NOTES

Saint-Saëns worked on the Organ Symphony at the same time as one of his lightest and brightest compositions, Le Carnaval des Animaux (The Carnival of the Animals). This is a particularly interesting example of how an artist can work on two totally different compositions simultaneously.

JEAN SIBELIUS *1865–1957*

Karelia Suite

OPUS 11: INTERMEZZO

This evocative music about Sibelius's Finnish homeland opens with the entire string section divided into many strands, as if depicting the rustling of countless leaves on a thousand trees. Meanwhile, the horns outline the sounds of a march, as though heard from the distance. Gradually, other instruments join in, louder and stronger until, led by the trumpets, the march is played in full as it passes. The strings then come into their own, tingling with excitement, as, eventually, the parade is over.

DISPUTED LAND

The history of Karelia *(right)*, a land of lakes, rocks, and dense forests, is complicated. When Sibelius wrote the *Karelia Suite*, it was part of Finland, which was a part of the old Russian Empire. Records of the region date as far back as 893 A.D. but Karelia was split up in 1917 when the newly formed Soviet Union—in return for granting full Finnish independence—swallowed up its eastern half. Western Karelia remained part of Finland until 1940 when it was claimed by Stalin in the aftermath of the Russo-Finnish war. Today Karelia forms part of the Russian Federation, although Finland continues to lay claim to it.

"OLD PFUND STERLING"

In 1921, Sibelius *(left)* attended a concert at the University of Birmingham. As well as Sibelius's *Voces Intimae*, the concert also featured a piano piece by a student, Laurence Powell. Afterward, Sibelius congratulated Powell, who told the composer: "I should like to go to London next week to hear you conduct your Fifth Symphony, but I cannot afford the rail fare." "Then I will give you ein pfund sterling," said Sibelius. This was a large amount of money for the time, so he became affectionately known as "Old Pfund Sterling."

KEY NOTES

Karelia is a plateau, rich in both lakes and folklore. In 1893, the year of Karelia's millennium, the Danish University of Viborg invited Sibelius to write the music to mark the occasion, part of which was the Karelia Suite.

RICHARD WAGNER
1813–1883

Lohengrin

ACT III (PRELUDE)

A sudden upward rush from the strings along with a thrilling tune from the trombones set this rousing music on its way. The trombone tune appears and reappears throughout the orchestra in varied guises, with gentler relief provided by a new theme on the woodwind. But it is the vibrant and animated tune that dominates all until, at the end, the music dies away to finish in an air of calm, peace, and quiet.

THE FIRST PERFORMANCE

 The first performance of Wagner's *Lohengrin*, the sixth of his thirteen operatic works, took place in 1850 in Weimar and was conducted by Franz Liszt. Wagner was not present because the previous year he had narrowly escaped arrest for his part in an uprising in Dresden. Sheltered by Liszt, he had fled to Zürich.

MARRIED LIAISONS

In 1863 Wagner fell in love with Cosima *(above, left)*, Liszt's daughter. At the time, however, she was married to the conductor and pianist Hans von Bülow. But Cosima left her husband for Wagner *(above, standing)*, by whom she had had three children. She eventually married him against Liszt's wishes. Liszt *(above, second right)*, despite his admiration for Wagner's genius and the fact that he too had fallen in love with a married woman, disapproved of the situation. He finally became reconciled to their love, but Cosima never fully forgave her father.

THE MYSTERIOUS LOHENGRIN

Lohengrin is about a knight who appears on a magic boat drawn by a swan. He has come to the aid of a young girl, Elsa, who is accused of murdering her brother. After winning a trial to clear her name, the knight proposes to her on the condition that Elsa never asks his name. But she is persuaded by the wife of her guardian to do just this in a plot to ruin the marriage. The knight kills the guardian and reveals himself to be Lohengrin *(below)*, a legendary knight of the Holy Grail. Unfortunately, with his identity revealed, he has to return to his brotherhood, and the magic boat and swan reappear. But before Lohengrin leaves his heartbroken bride, the swan changes form into Elsa's missing brother.

KEY NOTES

Wagner was keen on new developments in musical instruments. In his score for Lohengrin he asked for a bass clarinet, which had just been invented.

JOHANNES BRAHMS *1833–1897*

Academic Festival Overture

OPUS 80

*P*erhaps surprisingly, this colorful piece, which celebrates the joys of academic life, begins quietly and sedately in the bass. The mood is one of expectancy, calling to mind a group of people gathering together for a great occasion. But once the violins and horns have intoned their solemn tune, the opening begins to grow in power. The music soon breaks out joyfully, before building up to the old Latin tune *Gaudeamus igitur*, which brings the overture to a memorable conclusion with the full orchestra.

ACADEMIC HONOR

 In March 1879, when Brahms was forty-five, the University of Breslau granted him an Honorary Doctorate of Philosophy. In acknowledgment of the award, Brahms composed the *Academic Festival Overture*, the first of a contrasting pair of such works. It was first heard at a concert in Breslau on January 4, 1881 in a program which also included its companion piece, the *Tragic Overture, Opus 81*, as well as his Second Symphony.

A CONFIRMED BACHELOR

Brahms adored women and frequently fell in love but never married, preferring a bachelor's life. His humble beginnings, lack of formal schooling, and general lack of social polish made him awkward in the company of the grander ladies to whom his art gave him access. Yet he did have two great loves in his life—Agathe von Siebold and Clara *(right)*, widow of the composer Robert Schumann, both somewhat older than Brahms. Reputedly, it was the fear of losing his independence that convinced him that it was best not to marry under any circumstances.

UNIVERSITY AWARDS

The award of honorary degrees to composers became fashionable as the influence of the universities in the world of music began to grow from the mid-19th century onward. Brahms *(left)* was among several great masters who accepted such awards from European institutions. In England, the leading university to award honorary doctorates to composers was Cambridge, which exalted such famous names as Dvořák, Tchaikovsky, Grieg, and Bruch.

BRAHMS

KEY NOTES

In the Academic Festival Overture, *Brahms establishes a link with his youthful student audience by basing the music on popular student songs of the time. The first performance was reported to be "stormily applauded." The* Academic Festival Overture *has ranked among Brahms's most popular concert works ever since.*

GEORGE FRIDERIC HANDEL
1685–1759

The Water Music

HORNPIPE

The splendor of 18th-century majesty is heard in this section of Handel's masterpiece. A stately theme on the full Baroque orchestra leads to a brilliant faster section dominated by violins and a pair of oboes. It is a solo oboe that begins the slow final section of the hornpipe, both solemn and grand, as the floating procession pauses for a moment.

MUSIC ON THE WATER

Although there is a popular myth that *The Water Music* was written to appease King George I after Handel had taken an extended leave of absence from his employment, the idea for the piece probably came from the king himself, who wanted music for an evening river concert. It was performed on the Thames River in July 1717 with the orchestra performing from a group of barges.

KEY NOTES

The first performance of The Water Music proved to be so popular with King George I that he commanded it to be played twice more during the course of the evening!

The Celebrated WATER MUSICK in Seven Parts viz. Two FRENCH HORNS Two VIOLINS or HOBOYS a TENOR and a Thorough Bass for the HARPSICORD or BASS VIOLIN Compos'd by Mr. Handel

PYOTR TCHAIKOVSKY *1840–1893*

Symphony No.4 in F Minor

OPUS 36: FOURTH MOVEMENT

he opening music heralds a simple yet utterly memorable tune on the woodwinds. Though so typical of Tchaikovsky, this is, in fact, a folk tune that has been adapted for the full orchestra. The lyrical strings, triumphant brass, and dazzling woodwinds are all underpinned by a powerful percussion section which urges the music on to its grand conclusion.

STRONG FEELINGS

Tchaikovsky felt passionately about his *Symphony No.4*. Referring to it in correspondence, the composer spoke of "Fate...whose might is invincible." Of the fourth movement in particular, he wrote, "If you have had no pleasure in yourself, look about you. Go to the people: see how they can enjoy life...Rejoice in the happiness of others and you can still live."

KEY NOTES

This symphony was composed in 1877, the year of Tchaikovsky's ill-fated marriage to Antonina Milyukova, a young student who persuaded him to marry her. It is doubtful if there was any real love on his part, and Tchaikovsky actually dedicated the work to his benefactress, Nadezhda von Meck.

JOHANN SEBASTIAN BACH
1685–1750

Brandenburg Concerto No.2

THIRD MOVEMENT

The clarino trumpet leads the way in this lively and stimulating movement. This Baroque trumpet is supported by the strings and harpsichord before being answered by flutes and oboes. As the movement continues, each of the wind instruments takes its share of the limelight, until all combine in a final restatement of Bach's stirring and vivacious theme.

THE CLARINO TRUMPET

The last movement of the *Brandenburg Concerto No.2* is notable for its flamboyant writing for high clarino trumpet *(left)*. Smaller than the familiar trumpet, it was relatively common in Bach's day. Although it is not used in modern symphony orchestras, the recent interest in authentic period performance has led to a revival of this old instrument.

COURT COMPOSER

From 1717 to 1723, Bach served as court composer to Prince Leopold of Anhalt in the German town of Cöthen *(below)*. During this period, he wrote many of his orchestral works, including the six *Brandenburg Concertos*, which were commissioned by the Margrave of Brandenburg in 1721—hence their title. However, because the instruments used in the concertos varied greatly from those at the Margrave's disposal, the commission was ignored and Bach received no immediate reward for one of his most famous works.

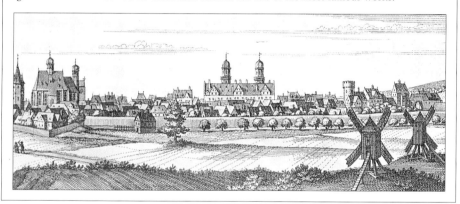

DOING TIME

Unfortunately, Bach was detained from taking up his new appointment at Cöthen on time. Disgruntled at losing such a musical talent, Bach's previous employer, the duke of Weimar, had him imprisoned for a month before he finally relented and allowed the composer to leave.

KEY NOTES

The Brandenburg Concertos are unusual in that each one is written for a different combination of instruments, and sometimes—notably No.5—for more than one solo instrument. Bach uses his soloists as if they were the main contributors in a conversation. The variety that he manages to extract from them shows his musical genius.

LUDWIG VAN BEETHOVEN
1770–1827

Symphony No. 9 in D Minor

OPUS 125, "CHORAL": FOURTH MOVEMENT

The finale to one of the most famous and memorable works ever written, the fourth movement to *Choral Symphony* introduces a great epic theme. The chorus enters grandly, singing a hymn to humanity. The voices muse upon the message in a moving passage of solemnity. Then it seems as if the entire world is caught up in an irresistible outpouring of celebration as all the instruments of the orchestra gradually join in. The theme increases in power as this epic symphony reaches its conclusion.

GRAND SYMPHONY

Beethoven completed *Symphony No.9* in February of 1824. At the time of its publication, it was the longest symphony ever written. Another one of his large-scale symphonies, his *Symphony No.10*—which he was working on at the time of his death in 1827—was intended to be a purely orchestral work, without voices.

POETIC INSPIRATION

An inspiration for the last movement of Beethoven's *Symphony No.9* was the German dramatist and poet Johann Christoph Friedrich von Schiller (1759–1805). His poem, *An die Freude* ("Ode to Joy") fired Beethoven's imagination in 1793, but it took the composer some thirty years before he finally set Schiller's verse to music in the *Choral*. Schiller *(right)* was not a musician himself, but his writings inspired many composers, including Rossini (*William Tell*) and Verdi (*Don Carlos*).

DEAFNESS

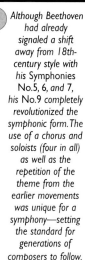

By the time that Ludwig van Beethoven *(left)* composed his *Symphony No.9*, he was completely deaf. He was present at the first performance, and when the music was over, he had to be turned round to face the cheering audience so he could witness their enthusiastic response to its recital, as he could not hear their tumultuous applause.

KEY NOTES

Although Beethoven had already signaled a shift away from 18th-century style with his Symphonies No.5, 6, and 7, his No.9 completely revolutionized the symphonic form. The use of a chorus and soloists (four in all) as well as the repetition of the theme from the earlier movements was unique for a symphony—setting the standard for generations of composers to follow.

Credits & Acknowledgments

PICTURE CREDITS

Cover /Title and Contents Pages/ IBC: Image Bank/Gary Gay

AKG London: 5, 7(tr), 17(br), 19(b); (A. Canaletto: Festival on the Thames): 20(tl), 21, 22(b), 23; Schiller-Nationalmuseum, Marbach: 25(tr); Bildarchiv Preussischer Kulturbesitz: 18; Bridgeman Art Library, London/Santa Corona/Vicenza (Giovanni Bellini: Baptism of Christ, St. John Altarpiece): 2; Chateau de Versailles (J. Nocret: The Family of Louis XIV): 3(t); Fitzwilliam Museum, University of Cambridge (A. Reichelt: Flowers Under a Lion Fountain): 8; Courtauld Institute Galleries, University of London (Manet: Bar at the Folies Bergères): 10(br); ©1997 Comstock: 15(b); E.T. Archive/V & A Museum, London: 5; Courtesy of The European Broadcasting Union: 4(b); Mary Evans Picture Library: 3(br), 6, 7(bl), 10(tl & tr), 11(t), 12, 13(bl); Hulton Getty: 7(br); Images Colour Library: 14, 22(tr); Lebrecht Collection: 11(b), 13(tr), 15(tl), 17(tl), 19(t), 20(bl), 25(bl); M-Press Picture Library: 4(t); Performing Arts Library/Clive Barda: 16, 24; Zefa: 9.

All illustrations and symbols: John See